Teaching Little Fingers to Play
Children's Songs
Piano Solos with Optional Teacher Accompaniments
Arranged by
Carolyn Miller

CONTENTS

Book
ISBN 978-1-4234-6755-7

Book/CD
ISBN 978-1-4234-6756-4

EXCLUSIVELY DISTRIBUTED BY

HAL•LEONARD®
CORPORATION
7777 W. BLUEMOUND RD. P.O. BOX 13819 MILWAUKEE, WI 53213

WILLIS MUSIC

Visit Hal Leonard Online at
www.halleonard.com

Hint!—

Find the measure where the left hand (L.H.) must cross over the right hand. Circle it so you remember!

Student Position

One octave higher when performing as a duet

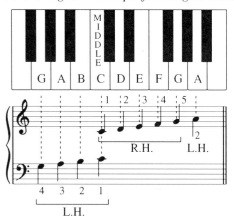

"C" Is for Cookie

Optional Teacher Accompaniment

Words and Music by Joe Raposo
Arranged by Carolyn Miller

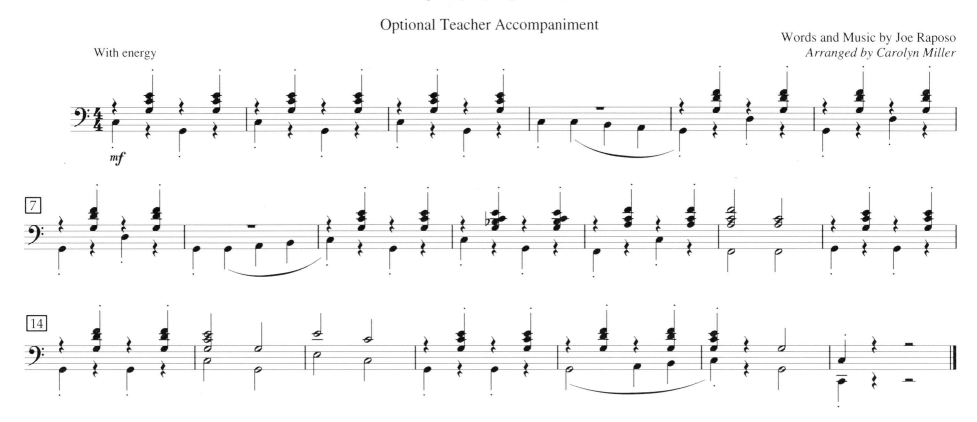

"C" Is for Cookie 1/2

Play both hands one octave higher when performing as a duet.

Words and Music by Joe Raposo
Arranged by Carolyn Miller

With energy

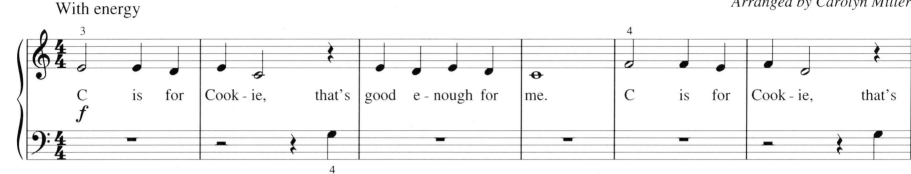

C is for Cook - ie, that's good e - nough for me. C is for Cook - ie, that's

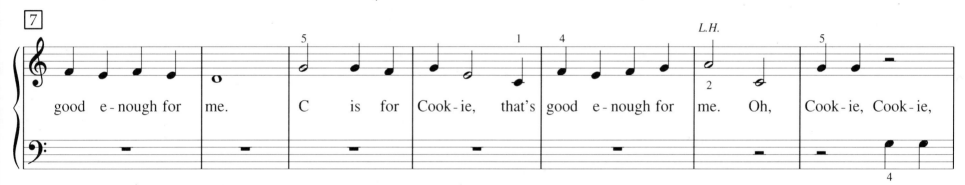

good e - nough for me. C is for Cook - ie, that's good e - nough for me. Oh, Cook - ie, Cook - ie,

Cook - ie starts with C. Cook - ie, Cook - ie, Cook - ie starts with C.

4

Hint!—
There are lots of ties in this very funny song. It would help to count out loud as you practice.

How many notes can you find that are held for

       7 beats? _____
       8 beats? _____

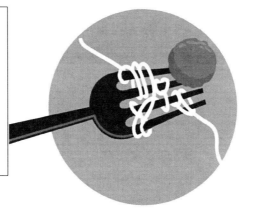

Student Position
One octave higher when performing as a duet

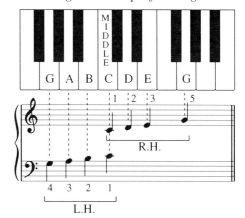

On Top of Spaghetti

Optional Teacher Accompaniment

Words and Music by Tom Glazer
Arranged by Carolyn Miller

Moderately, like a waltz

mp

On Top of Spaghetti

Play both hands one octave higher when performing as a duet.

Words and Music by Tom Glazer
Arranged by Carolyn Miller

Moderately, like a waltz

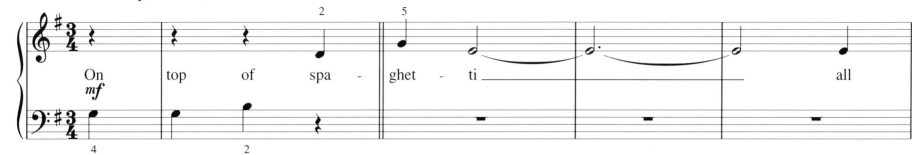

On top of spa - ghet - ti _____ all

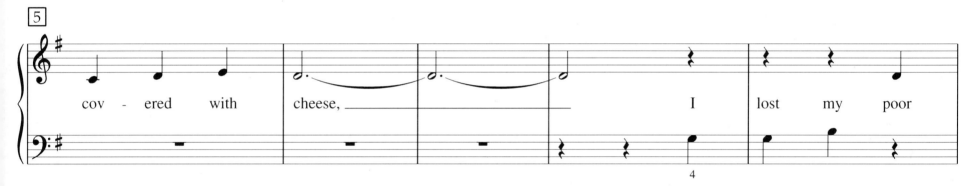

cov - ered with cheese, _____ I lost my poor

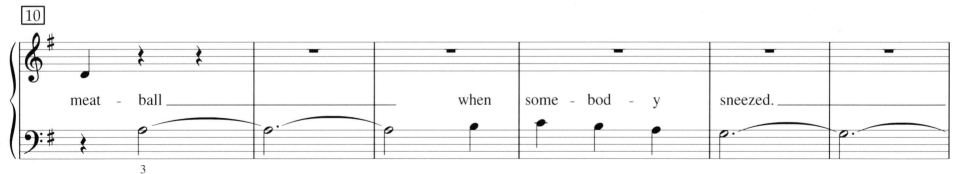

meat - ball _____ when some - bod - y sneezed. _____

Optional Teacher Accompaniment

7

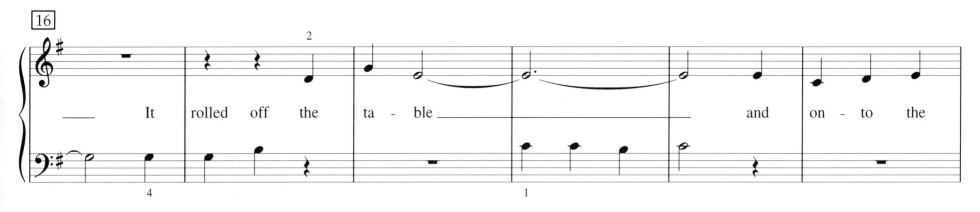

It rolled off the ta - ble _____ and on - to the

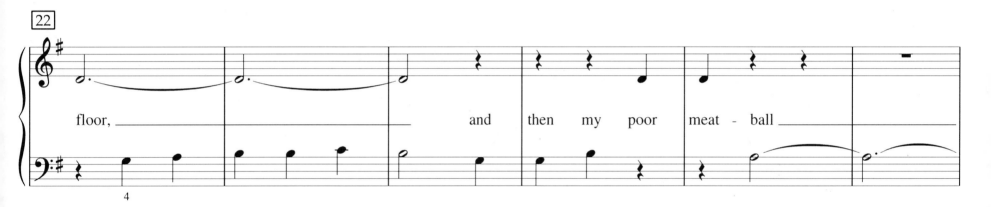

floor, _____ and then my poor meat - ball _____

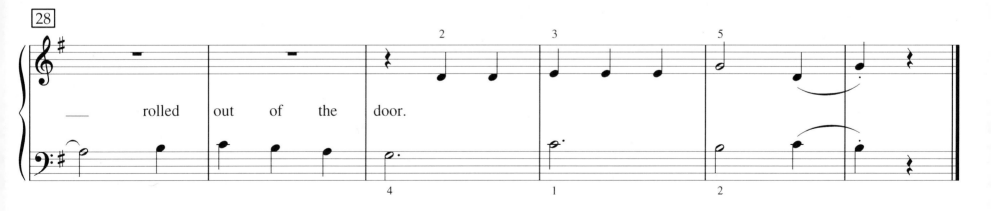

_____ rolled out of the door.

Remember—

When a flat sign (♭) or sharp sign (♯) is placed between the clef sign and the time signature, it becomes the *Key Signature*. In this piece the flat is positioned on the B line which turns all B's in this song to B-flats. The key of the piece is F Major.

Count the number of B-flats in the left hand: _____

Student Position

One octave higher when performing as a duet

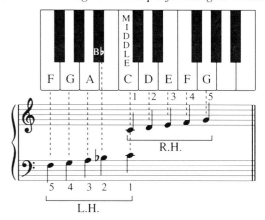

Puff the Magic Dragon

Optional Teacher Accompaniment

Words and Music by Lenny Lipton and Peter Yarrow
Arranged by Carolyn Miller

Puff the Magic Dragon

Words and Music by Lenny Lipton and Peter Yarrow
Arranged by Carolyn Miller

Play both hands one octave higher when performing as a duet.

Dreamily, not too fast

Hint!—
Practice playing the F Major scale up *and* down before playing this song.

Now try these variations of the scale.
Play each note:

- 2 times each
- 3 times each
- very softly
- as LOUD as possible!

Student Position
One octave higher when performing as a duet

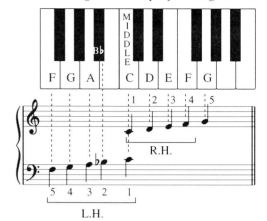

How Much Is That Doggie in the Window
Optional Teacher Accompaniment

Words and Music by Bob Merrill
Arranged by Carolyn Miller

Happily, like a waltz

How Much Is That Doggie in the Window

Play both hands one octave higher when performing as a duet.

Words and Music by Bob Merrill
Arranged by Carolyn Miller

Happily, like a waltz

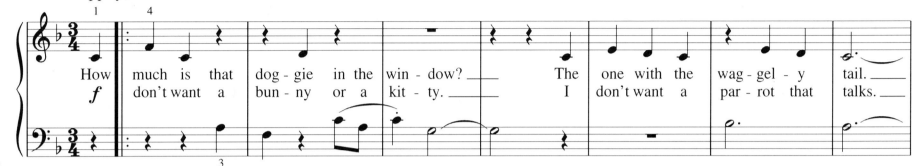

How much is that dog-gie in the win-dow? ___ The one with the wag-gel-y tail. ___
don't want a bun-ny or a kit-ty. ___ I don't want a par-rot that talks.

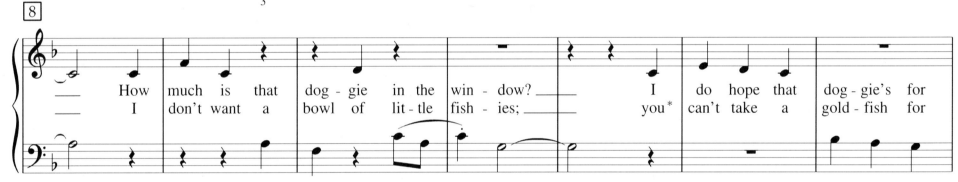

___ How much is that dog-gie in the win-dow? ___ I do hope that dog-gie's for
___ I don't want a bowl of lit-tle fish-ies; ___ you* can't take a gold-fish for

1. sale. ___ I **2.** walks. ___ *cresc.* *ff*

*original: "he"

Hint!—
This piece is in G Major. Play the G Major scale up and down a few times before beginning this piece.

Student Position
One octave higher when performing as a duet

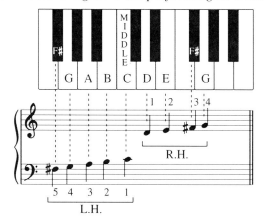

Lavender Blue
(Dilly Dilly)
from Walt Disney's SO DEAR TO MY HEART

Optional Teacher Accompaniment

Words by Larry Morey
Music by Eliot Daniel
Arranged by Carolyn Miller

Lavender Blue

9/10

(Dilly Dilly)

from Walt Disney's SO DEAR TO MY HEART

Words by Larry Morey
Music by Eliot Daniel
Arranged by Carolyn Miller

Play both hands one octave higher when performing as a duet.

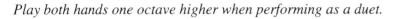

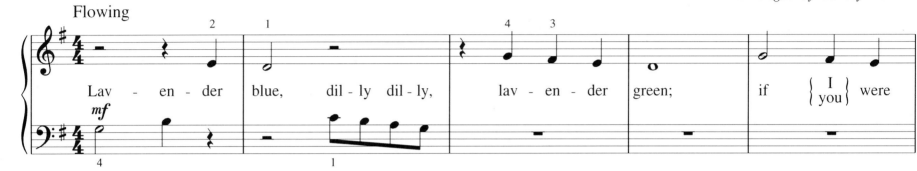

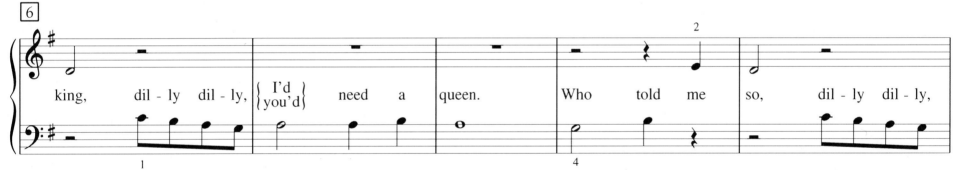

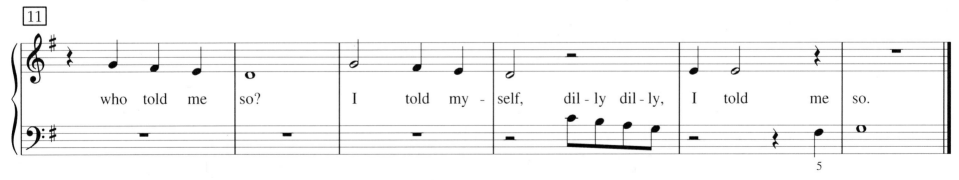

14

Reminders—
- a natural (♮) cancels a sharp or flat
- a sharped note remains sharped throughout the measure unless a natural is placed before it

How many D♯'s are in measure 5? _____
How many D♯'s are in measure 6? _____

Student Position

One octave higher when performing as a duet

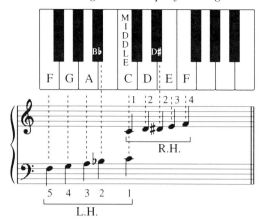

The Hokey Pokey

Optional Teacher Accompaniment

Words and Music by Charles P. Macak,
Tafft Baker and Larry LaPrise
Arranged by Carolyn Miller

With energy (♩♪ = ♩♪)

mp

f

The Hokey Pokey

Words and Music by Charles P. Macak,
Tafft Baker and Larry LaPrise
Arranged by Carolyn Miller

Play both hands one octave higher when performing as a duet.

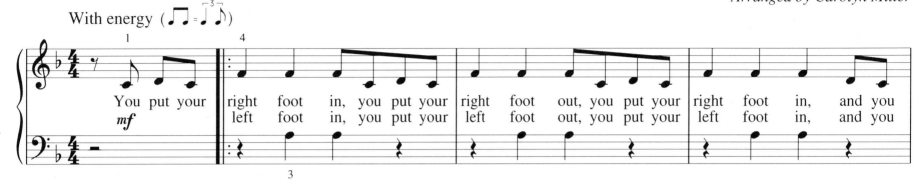

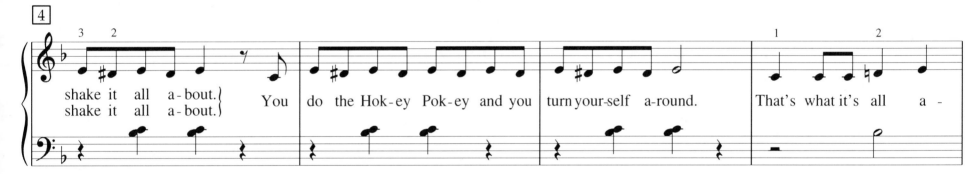

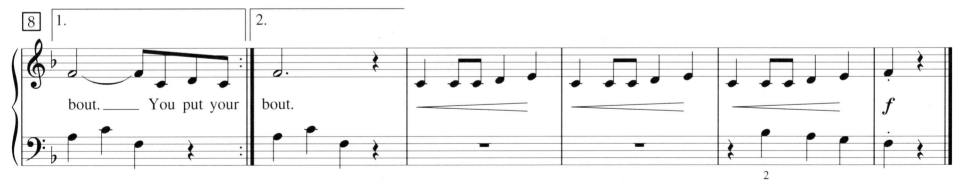

Practice Tip—
Play this with your L.H.:

See if you can find the notes in the song.

Student Position
One octave higher when performing as a duet

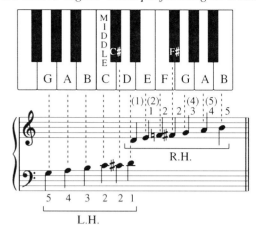

Sing
from SESAME STREET

Optional Teacher Accompaniment

Words and Music by Joe Raposo
Arranged by Carolyn Miller

Sing
from SESAME STREET

Words and Music by Joe Raposo
Arranged by Carolyn Miller

Play both hands one octave higher when performing as a duet.

Moderately, with a bounce

18

Optional Teacher Accompaniment

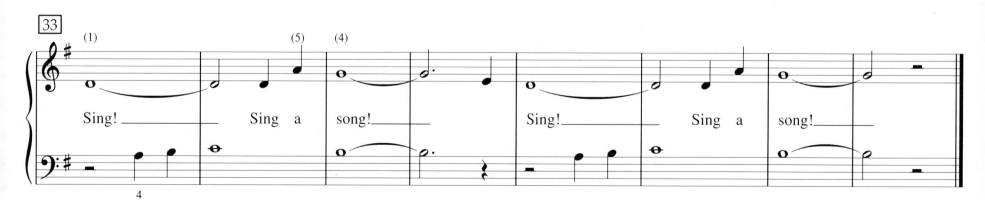

Practice Tip!—
Study this rhythm carefully. It's really cool!

$\frac{4}{4}$ 𝅘𝅥 𝅘𝅥𝅮𝅘𝅥𝅮𝅘𝅥𝅮 𝅘𝅥 | 𝅘𝅥 𝅘𝅥𝅮𝅘𝅥𝅮𝅘𝅥𝅮 𝅘𝅥

Tap it on the fallboard before starting to play.

Investigate!—
Measure 3 is echoed in measure 4. Which measure is softer? Does this echo happen again? Where?

Student Position

One octave higher when performing as a duet

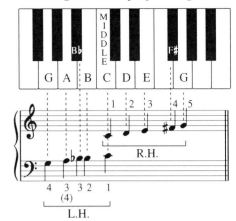

Elmo's Song

Optional Teacher Accompaniment

Words and Music by Tony Geiss
Arranged by Carolyn Miller

Elmo's Song

Words and Music by Tony Geiss
Arranged by Carolyn Miller

Play both hands one octave higher when performing as a duet.

Quickly, happily

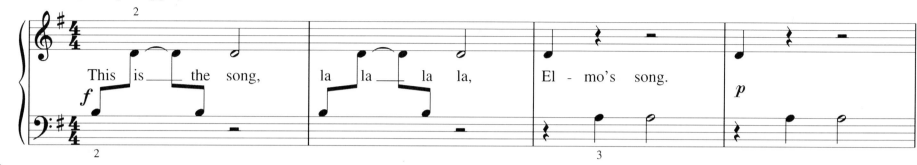

This is the song, la la la la, El - mo's song.

La la la la la la la la, El - mo's song. La la la la la la

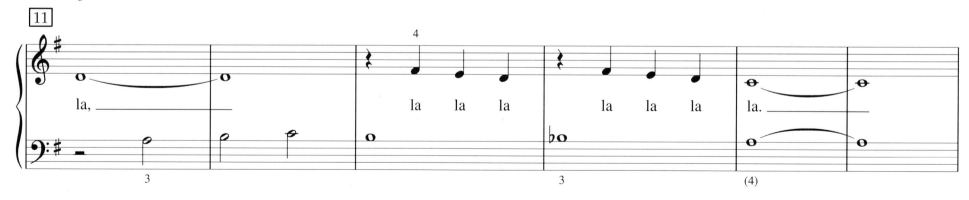

la, la la la la la la la.

Optional Teacher Accompaniment

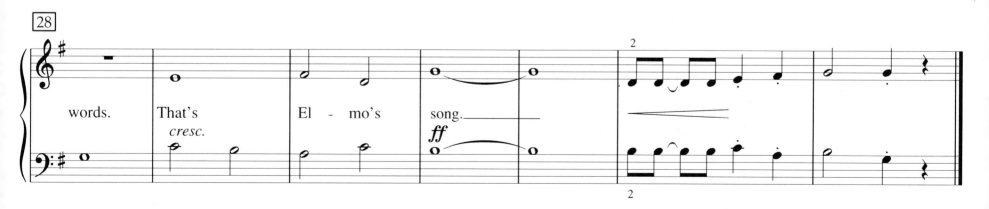

Tip!—

There are two different sections to this piece: the A section and the B section. The B section, which usually sounds very different from the A section, is "sandwiched" between two A sections:

A – B – A

A song in this format is usually said to be in "ABA form."

See if you can find the exact measure where the A section returns!

Student Position

One octave higher when performing as a duet

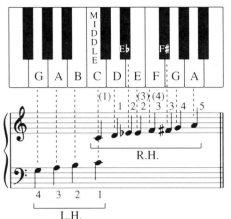

Rumbly in My Tumbly
from Walt Disney's THE MANY ADVENTURES OF WINNIE THE POOH

Optional Teacher Accompaniment

Words and Music by Richard M. Sherman
and Robert B. Sherman
Arranged by Carolyn Miller

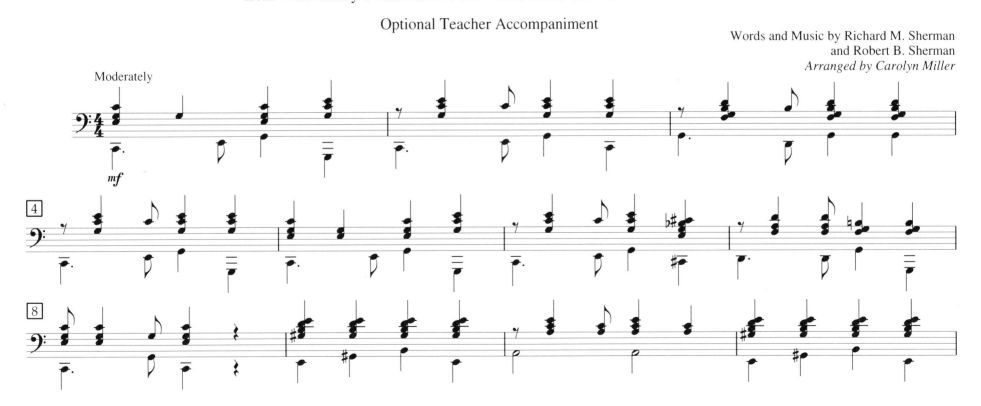

Rumbly in My Tumbly

from Walt Disney's THE MANY ADVENTURES OF WINNIE THE POOH

Words and Music by Richard M. Sherman
and Robert B. Sherman
Arranged by Carolyn Miller

Play both hands one octave higher when performing as a duet.

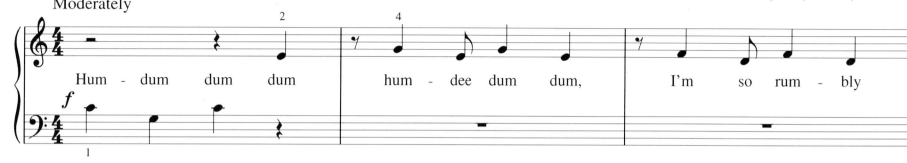

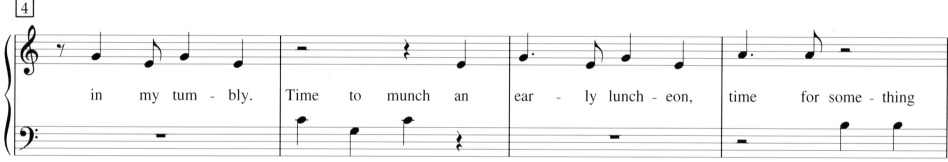

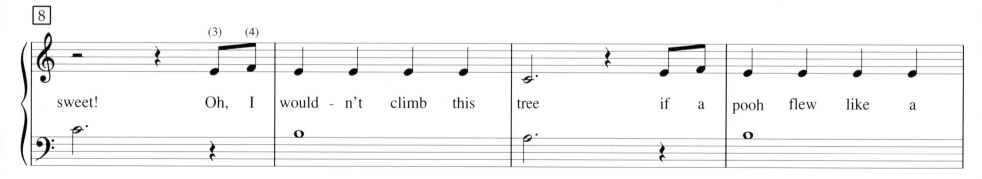

Optional Teacher Accompaniment

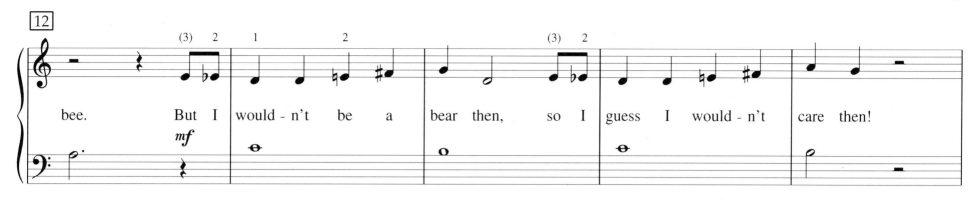

Hint!—
Pay careful attention to the hand position changes that occur throughout this piece, and especially at measures 21 and 24.

Student Position
One octave higher when performing as a duet

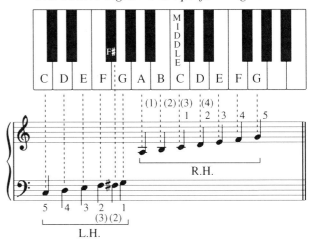

Any Dream Will Do
from JOSEPH AND THE AMAZING TECHNICOLOR® DREAMCOAT

Optional Teacher Accompaniment

Music by Andrew Lloyd Webber
Lyrics by Tim Rice
Arranged by Carolyn Miller

Any Dream Will Do

from JOSEPH AND THE AMAZING TECHNICOLOR® DREAMCOAT

19/20

Music by Andrew Lloyd Webber
Lyrics by Tim Rice
Arranged by Carolyn Miller

Play both hands one octave higher when performing as a duet.

Optional Teacher Accompaniment

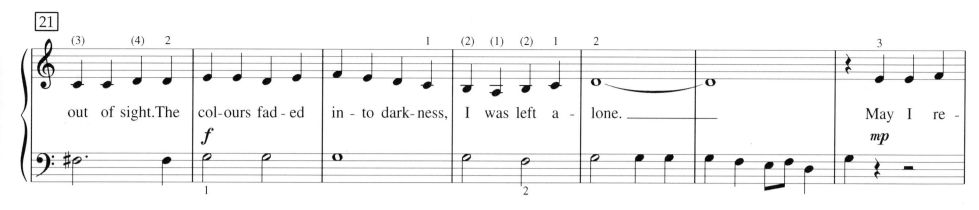

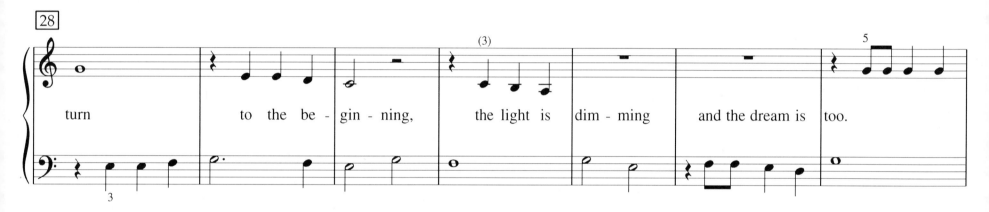

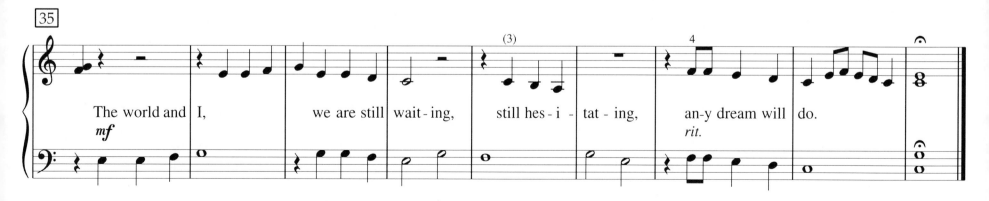

TEACHING LITTLE FINGERS TO PLAY

TEACHING LITTLE FINGERS TO PLAY

by John Thompson

A series for the early beginner combining rote and note approach. The melodies are written with careful thought and are kept as simple as possible, yet they are refreshingly delightful. All the music lies within the grasp of the child's small hands.

00412076 Book only $6.99
00406523 Book/Audio $9.99

TEACHING LITTLE FINGERS TO PLAY ENSEMBLE

by John Thompson

A book of intermediate-level accompaniments for use in the teacher's studio or at home. Two possible accompaniments are included for each *Teaching Little Fingers* piece: a Secondo or Primo part, as well as a second piano part for studios that have two pianos/keyboards.

00412228 Book only $6.99

DISNEY TUNES

arr. Glenda Austin

10 delightful Disney songs: The Bare Necessities • Can You Feel the Love Tonight • Candle on the Water • God Help the Outcasts • Kiss the Girl • Mickey Mouse March • The Siamese Cat Song • Winnie the Pooh • You'll Be in My Heart (Pop Version) • Zip-A-Dee-Doo-Dah.

00416748 Book only $9.99
00416749 Book/Audio $12.99

CHRISTMAS CAROLS

arr. Carolyn Miller

12 piano solos: Angels We Have Heard on High • Deck the Hall • The First Noel • Hark! The Herald Angels Sing • Jingle Bells • Jolly Old Saint Nicholas • Joy to the World! • O Come, All Ye Faithful • O Come Little Children • Silent Night • Up on the Housetop • We Three Kings of Orient Are.

00406391 Book only $7.99
00406722 Book/Audio $10.99

CLASSICS

arr. Randall Hartsell

11 piano classics: Bridal Chorus (from *Lohengrin*) (Wagner) • Can-Can (from *Orpheus in the Underworld*) (Offenbach) • Country Gardens (English Folk Tune) • A Little Night Music (from *Eine kleine Nachtmusik*) (Mozart) • Lullaby (Brahms) • Ode to Joy (from Symphony No. 9) (Beethoven) • Symphony No. 5 (Second Movement) (Tchaikovsky) • and more.

00406550 Book only $7.99
00406736 Book/Audio $10.99

HYMNS

arr. Mary K. Sallee

11 hymns: Amazing Grace • Faith of Our Fathers • For the Beauty of the Earth • Holy, Holy, Holy • Jesus Loves Me • Jesus Loves the Little Children • Joyful, Joyful, We Adore Thee • Kum Bah Yah • Praise Him, All Ye Little Children • We Are Climbing Jacob's Ladder • What a Friend We Have in Jesus.

00406413 Book only $7.99
00406731 Book/Audio $10.99

TEACHING LITTLE FINGERS TO PLAY MORE

by Leigh Kaplan

Teaching Little Fingers to Play More is a fun-filled and colorfully illustrated follow-up book to *Teaching Little Fingers to Play*. This book strengthens skills learned while easing the transition into John Thompson's *Modern Course, Book One*.

00406137 Book only $6.99
00406527 Book/Audio $10.99

MORE DISNEY TUNES

arr. Glenda Austin

9 songs, including: Circle of Life • Colors of the Wind • A Dream Is a Wish Your Heart Makes • A Spoonful of Sugar • Under the Sea • A Whole New World • and more.

00416750 Book only $9.99
00416751 Book/Audio $12.99

MORE EASY DUETS

arr. Carolyn Miller

9 more fun duets arranged for 1 piano, 4 hands: A Bicycle Built for Two (Daisy Bell) • Blow the Man Down • Chopsticks • Do Your Ears Hang Low? • I've Been Working on the Railroad • The Man on the Flying Trapeze • Short'nin' Bread • Skip to My Lou • The Yellow Rose of Texas.

00416832 Book only $7.99
00416833 Book/Audio $10.99

MORE BROADWAY SONGS

arr. Carolyn Miller

10 more fantastic Broadway favorites arranged for a young performer, including: Castle on a Cloud • Climb Ev'ry Mountain • Gary, Indiana • In My Own Little Corner • It's the Hard-Knock Life • Memory • Oh, What a Beautiful Mornin' • Sunrise, Sunset • Think of Me • Where Is Love?

00416928 Book only $6.99
00416929 Book/Audio $12.99

MORE CHILDREN'S SONGS

arr. Carolyn Miller

10 songs: The Candy Man • Do-Re-Mi • I'm Popeye the Sailor Man • It's a Small World • Linus and Lucy • The Muppet Show Theme • My Favorite Things • Sesame Street Theme • Supercalifragilisticexpialidocious • Tomorrow.

00416810 Book only $7.99
00416811 Book/Audio $12.99

WILLIS MUSIC

EXCLUSIVELY DISTRIBUTED BY

HAL•LEONARD®

7777 W. BLUEMOUND RD. P.O. BOX 13819
MILWAUKEE, WISCONSIN 53213

Prices, contents, and availability subject to change without notice.
Disney characters and artwork TM & © 2020 Disney

All arrangements come with optional teacher accompaniments.

FOR A COMPLETE SERIES LISTING, VISIT WWW.HALLEONARD.COM